The *A-Z* Wardrobe

A COMPACT GUIDE TO TIMELESS PIECES
EVERY WOMAN SHOULD OWN FOR
EFFORTLESS STYLE

Elsie Szto

Copyright © 2016 Elsie Szto.
All rights reserved. No part of this book may be reproduced, stored in a retrieval system, or transmitted in any form or by any means - electronic, mechanical, photocopy, recording, scanning, or otherwise - without the prior written permission of the author.
Meet Elsie online at www.butterfliesandmarigolds.com

National Library Board, Singapore Cataloguing-in-Publication Data
Name : Szto, Elsie, author.

Description: The A-Z wardrobe : a compact guide to timeless pieces every woman should own for effortless style / Elsie Szto. | Singapore: Elsie Szto, ©2015. | pages cm.

Identifiers : OCN 922948902 | ISBN 978-981-09-6726-0 (hardback) | ISBN 978-981-09-6727-7 (paperback) | ISBN 978-981-09-6728-4 (eBook)

Subject : Clothing and dress. | Beauty, Personal. | Fashion.
Classification: LC Classification TT507 | DDC 646.34 -- dc23

ISBN 978-981-09-6726-0 hardback
ISBN 978-981-09-6727-7 paperback
ISBN 978-981-09-6728-4 eBook

Contents

A 7
   A-Line Dress 8
   Animal Print 10
B 11
   Ballet Flats 12
   Belts 13
   Boots 15
C 17
   Cocktail Rings 18
   Cardigans 19
   Cashmere Wraps 21
   Cashmere Trivia 21
D 23
   Diamonds 24
   Diamond Trivia 24
   Denim 27
E 29
   Evening Gown 30
   Embellishments 32
F 35
   Fishnet Stockings 37
   Flannel Shirt 38
G 39
   Graphic Tees 40
   Gold 42
H 43
   Hoop Earrings 44
   High-Heeled Shoes 45
I 49
   Inspiration and Investment Items 50

J 53
    Jeans 54
    Jewel Tone Colors 56
K 59
    Khaki Trousers 60
    Knits 62
L 65
    Lace 66
    Little Black Dress 68
M 71
    Man's White Shirt 72
    Mary Janes 74
N 77
    Nude 78
    Necklaces 81
O 83
    Opaque Tights 84
P 87
    Pencil Skirt 88
    Pearls 89
Q 91
    Quirky Prints 92
    Quilted Jackets 95
R 97
    Red Lipstick 98
    R is for Rompers 100
S 103
    Sunglasses 104
    Suit 105
T 107
    T-Shirt 108
    Tuxedo 110

U 111
    Underwear 112
    Umbrella 113
V 115
    Voluminous Skirt 116
    Vintage 117
W 119
    Watch 120
    Wrap Dress 121
    Wedges 122
X 127
    X-Factor 1 128
    X-Factor 2 130
Y 131
    Yoga Wear 132
Z 137
    Zippered Hoodies 138

Dedication

For my family, who love me as I am, and always encourage me to chase my rainbow wherever it leads me. It is my greatest life's blessing and joy to have you as my own.

Author's Note

Hi there! My name is Elsie Szto and I am a fashion entrepreneur. I have been in the fashion business for more than 2 decades, having worked my way around the industry from salary clerk, merchandiser, fashion coordinator, buyer, brand manager and finally fulfilling my dream of running my own fashion business and an online store in Singapore where I reside.

I was always fascinated and passionate about fashion, pouring all my pocket money into fashion magazines - I loved reading about the latest trends and watching stylish women strut their stuff on fashion runways on television. However, because family finances were tight, my sister and I could only afford to get our hair cut and permed once a year, usually before Lunar New Year. I'd always end up with the same mushroom hairstyle that I hated! Mum would buy two outfits each for us and a pair of going-out shoes; usually white, because according to mum, white goes with everything. Till this day, I have a phobia for white shoes!

Necessity is the mother of invention and I learned to be very creative and resourceful in my formative years. Vain as I was, I learned quickly to stretch my shopping dollars, mix and match my new and old pieces, borrowing from my friends' wardrobes constantly to breathe new life into my very limited collection. I've torn jeans to simulate the distressed look, cut and dyed T-shirts, sewn sequins and lace on gowns, knitted my own sweaters, stuck glitter on blouses and made my own necklaces. At one point I even made my own beads from paper mache!

In my years in the fashion industry, I watched and admired stylish women I've met in the course of my work. I observe their style the way some kids study how to crack the latest video games. As a fashion buyer for a department store and a brand manager for a luxury label, I read sales numbers every day, and analysed (to death) why some styles sell out and some don't. Over time, I've come to realize that there are very valid reasons why certain pieces, colors and styles are popular with most women while others end up on the clearance racks. As I wear these pieces myself, over time, they have become my style anchors, onto which I am free to add fun and seasonal pieces for variety and freshness.

That's how this book came about. It's a compact guide of the key pieces I feel should be in every woman's wardrobe. They will simplify your morning dressing routine by leaps and bounds and give you added confidence and energy to face your day with grace, gladness and style!

XXX elsie

Forward

I believe that personal style is all about "self expression". Show me a stylish woman and I'll show you a woman who is confident in who she is and how she wants to show up in her world everyday. I believe great style comes from the congruence of recognizing who you are on the inside, and dressing up authentically to display that inner beauty to the world.

The items listed in this book form my foundation for a smart and stylish wardrobe. Independent of fashion trends that have come and gone, these are my essentials that have stood the test of time. They are my style vitamins, my list of 'go-to's. Whenever I'm expecting a challenging day and need a confidence booster; these are my pillars. I depend on them to carry me through, and they work like a charm – ALWAYS!

This book took a long time to come together because the process of writing made me feel very vulnerable at times, as if I invited you into my personal wardrobe and unveiled my private space. It is an intimate sharing of my thoughts, my choices and why each piece has a special place in my wardrobe.

It is by no means an exhaustive list. In fact, I'm sure this list will evolve, get edited with the passing of time, and the accumulation of my own life experiences. I'm already bubbling with excitement to see what new adventures are in store. At this point though, I am simply sharing my thoughts with you, having been blessed to watch and learn from the style blazers that have gone before.

I would be most honored if you would join me on this journey.

with grace, gladness & style.

"Above all, be the heroine of your life, not the victim."

Nora Ephron

A-Line Dress

Did you know that the A-line dress was created by Christian Dior in 1955? A-line dresses are named as such because they are narrower on top and flare out at the hem, resembling the capital letter "A". They were the most popular silhouette in Paris in the 1950's. They were worn by style icons in the 60's and 70's, such as Twiggy and Mary Quant and have remained popular to this day.

I feel that this dress should be in every smart woman's closet because the cut is incredibly flattering, especially for disguising bottom-heavy figures. It's really a dress for all seasons. In spring, wear the A-line dress with ballet flats or strappy sandals and in winter, pair it with opaque tights and boots. Both options are easy to create, comfortable and stylish.

In fact, this A-line silhouette works with solid colors, color-blocking and even abstract prints! My only caution would be to stay away from stripes - both horizontal or vertical. You want to avoid looking like a triangle!

Animal Print

Animal print, particularly leopard print, is timeless. It never goes out of style. In the past, animal skins were considered rather exotic and expensive and often flaunted as a symbol of wealth and status.

As the story goes, Oleg Cassini made an exquisite coat out of leopard pelts for First Lady Jacqueline Kennedy in 1961, and scores of ladies copied the look. The rest, as they say, is history.

When wearing animal print, remember the age-old adage, "LESS IS MORE". I recommend wearing only ONE animal print item at a time. In my opinion, animal print is neutral but wild; in my book that means animal print goes with everything! That said, I feel that the best way to wear animal print is to let the print take centre stage and keep everything else that you are wearing chic and simple.

If the thought of wearing an animal print dress or blouse intimidates you, why not try the print out in an accent accessory, like a pair of ballet flats, a clutch bag, a skinny belt or even a hair band? Take a risk, walk on the wild side!

"Be yourself,
no matter what they say."

Sting

Ballet Flats

Ballet flats have been around since the 18th century and are rightly named as they were originally fashioned for pointe ballerinas. The usage changed drastically in 1956, when Brigitte Bardot, who was actually trained as a ballet dancer, asked French Label Repetto to make her a pair of flats for her mambo dance scene in "And God Created Woman". After the film's debut, both Brigitte Bardot and her crimson ballet flats became overnight sensations.

As if that was not ammunition enough, a year later, Audrey Hepburn wore her pair of ballet flats for her dance scene in the movie "Funny Face", and ballet flats became the most fashionable flat shoe every woman should own ever since!

Ballet flats are chic and comfortable, making them the supreme shoe choice for errand day and running about town. You can never go wrong with a patent black pair, but I think it would be fun to add a bold color or 2 or 3 to brighten up your wardrobe. It would also be interesting to look out for ballet flats in exotic skins, like leopard, ostrich or python or get a pair in metallic colors for texture and some serious bling.

Belts

History records that belts have been worn by men since the Bronze Age. In the 16th century, belts were worn in the military as bands around the waist to hold weapons in place and to hold one's pants up at the same time. By the 1850s, belts infiltrated women's styles when dresses were adorned with sashes made in matching fabrics.

Belts are a quick and easy way to give definition to the waist. Unfortunately, belts are often overlooked and under-utilized as a fashion accessory, when in fact, wearing the right belt will make us look slimmer and accentuate our curves.

Choose belts with interesting buckles, textured leather or animal print so that they stand out on their own like a fashion accessory (not an afterthought). These days, skinny belts are intentionally longer, so an interesting and modern way to wear them is to single or double loop them around the body, after you have buckled the belt. This prevents the belt from flapping excessively against the body, especially if there are no belt loops on the clothes to hold the belt down properly.

Boots

I admit it. I've got a thing for boots. Cowboy boots, ankle boots, thigh-high Pretty Woman boots. I just think boots are incredibly sexy footwear period.

If you are new to boots, try them with jeans for starters, then promote yourself to A-line mini dresses with opaque tights and cow-boy boots or ankle boots. I believe one should invest in a pair of quality boots and not worry about getting them worn in. They should look a little rugged and aged, that's when they become super comfy, like a familiar old friend. Boots are comfort food for your feet so invest well, choose wisely and indulge often.

Yee-Ha!

"Clothes make the man. Naked people have little or no influence in society."

Mark Twain

Cocktail Rings

I love to see a woman accessorize with drama and a fun way to do that is with an oversized cocktail ring. It makes for a great fashion statement, glams up any outfit instantly and is a great conversation starter at a party.

The cocktail ring doesn't have to be real (or a family heirloom). Try rings with semi-precious stones, or go vintage shopping and hunt them down at flea markets. Since this is intended to be a statement piece, give it space, wear ONE at a time, and keep other jewelry like earrings and necklaces minimal so that the cocktail ring gets the full exposure and attention it deserves.

Cardigans

The modern day cardigan got its name from the 7th Earl of Cardigan, Major General James Thomas Brudenell, who was a British Officer serving in the Crimea (modern-day Ukraine). In 1854, when the United Kingdom was battling Russia over the territory of the declining Ottoman Empire in what is known as the Crimean campaign, Brudenell and his officers wore a type of "sweater coat" that is now known as the cardigan (The History of the Cardigan Sweater, www.ehow.com).

These days, cardigans have become a key piece of clothing in every smart woman's wardrobe. Wear them as part of a twinset, or pair them with khakis and jeans. Push the style envelope further and wear cardigans over pencil skirts or over a fitted tee for a casual-I-just-threw-this-on-look. Super modern, super comfy, super chic. Look for interesting weaves, yarns, textures, or details so that your cardigan becomes a remarkable item, not just a wardrobe staple.

Cashmere Wraps

I love cashmere. There! I've said it! I live in the tropical island of Singapore where it's 30 degrees Celsius all year round and yes, I love cashmere!

Cashmere conjures images of sophistication and pure bliss. Cashmere feels super luxurious. As far as I know, it is the warmest of all natural fibers, and it gives coziness without the bulk. In fact, high quality cashmere can be up to eight times warmer than sheep's wool, despite its light weight. That's why a cashmere wrap or cardigan is the perfect travel appendage. It always keeps you warm and cosy in airports and flights without compromising on the style factor.

You wouldn't need that many, and if you take care of your cashmere properly, it will last, so allow yourself to spend a little more on your favourite neutral shade. I believe solid color is better than print, but that's just my personal opinion.

Cashmere Trivia

Cashmere has been manufactured in Nepal and Kashmir for thousands of years. The founder of the cashmere wool industry is traditionally thought to have been the 15th century ruler of Kashmir, Zain-ul-Abidin, who introduced weavers from Turkestan (modern day Turkey). (Wikipedia).

Cashmere is expensive because of its costly production process and its scarcity. It takes more than 2 cashmere goats to make a single 2-ply sweater. The fibers of the warming undercoat must be separated from a coarser protective top coat during the spring molting season, a labour-intensive process that typically involves combing and sorting the hair by hand. These factors contribute to the relatively low global production rate of cashmere – approximately 6,500 metric tons of pure cashmere annually, as opposed to 2 million metric tons of sheep's wool. (Aisha Harris, Why Is Cashmere More Expensive Than Other Kinds of Wool?, 2012)

The most expensive cashmere fibers come from the soft undercoat of Mongolia's mountain goats. Arguably, the best production house for cashmere is Loro Piano, the 200-year-old Italian company which has a mill outside of Milan and a herd of white caprahircus goats in Inner Mongolia (Sabrina Azadi, Tribune Newapapers, 17 Jan 2010). These days, most mass market retailers from JCrew, Banana Republic, Uniqlo and Marks & Spencer have hopped on the cashmere bandwagon, so simply pick one (or 10!) that meets your needs and matches your budget.

"Dress like you are embracing life,
not hiding from it."

Peter Morrisey

Diamonds

According to Marilyn Monroe, "Diamonds are a girl's best friend", and I dare say she was right! Seriously though, I can't think of many (any) outfits that "can't go" with a pair of diamond studs. Whether they are real or fake is immaterial! Of course, if you intend to buy the real thing, make sure you do your own research and due diligence. Always, buy from a reputable jeweler.

From a style perspective, diamond studs are the perfect understatement accessories. They add sparkle and class without being overtly ostentatious. They are perfect for day or night, spring or winter, casual or dressy occasions. To me, they are perfect for any occasion!

Diamond Trivia

The word 'diamond' comes from the Greek word Adamas, meaning "unbreakable", "proper" or "unalterable". They've been used as decorative items since ancient times and some of the earliest references can be traced to India. (Wikipedia).

Diamonds are valued (according to Wikipedia), by the *4C's* as follows:

- ***Carat weight***, which measures the mass of a diamond. One carat equals 200 milligrams. All things being equal, the price per carat increases with carat weight, since larger diamonds are both rarer and more desirable for use as gemstones.

- *Clarity* is the measure of internal defects of a diamond, called inclusions. Inclusions may be crystals of a foreign material or another diamond crystal, or even structural imperfections such as tiny cracks that can appear whitish or cloudy.
- *Color* is the 3rd C. The best color grading for diamonds is "D", which means the diamond is totally colorless. Diamonds with unusual or intense colorations are labeled as "fancy" diamonds. These colored diamonds in shades of pink, blue and yellow are rare and highly sought after too.
- *Cut* - the quality of a diamond's cut is widely considered the most important of the 4Cs. The skill with which a diamond is cut determines its ability to reflect and refract light. It is recognized that a well-cut diamond can appear to be of greater carat weight, and has clarity and color appear to be of better grade than it actually is. Diamonds are cut into a variety of shapes that are designed to accentuate the fire and brilliance of the gemstones. The most common shape is a round brilliant shape. Other cuts include: the Baguette (French, meaning a loaf of bread), Marquise, Heart, Pear, Princess cut (square outline) and Briolette.

Denim

Denim has come a long way since blue jeans were invented by Jacob Davis in 1871 and later patented by Levi Strauss in 1873 (Wikipedia). This humble cotton fabric has come a long way from its cowboys and miner days. Screen legends such as John Wayne, Marlon Brandon, Marilyn Monroe, and Brooke Shields, just to name a few, have all given their nod of approval to this humble fabric, turning it into a fashion industry staple to this day with no signs of slowing down.

These days, denim is not just for jeans and dungarees but also jackets, dresses, and shorts too! There are so many shades and washes to choose from and every designer has a denim 'something' in their collection. I am partial to classic blue denim. I like them dark for dressier occasions and appropriately worn out (in all the right places), frayed and slashed for casual weekends. As a general rule of thumb, wear only ONE denim item at any given time. The denim tuxedo is a huge NO-NO, even the cowboys don't do that anymore!

"Elegance is not about being noticed,
it's about being remembered."

Giorgio Armani

Evening Gown

Every smart woman knows that the hunt for the perfect evening gown begins when it's not needed. Its funny how watching the Academy Awards, Golden Globe Awards or any other red carpet shows have become a global pastime for critiquing celebrities in their evening gowns and there are lots programs featuring expert opinions of "who wore it best". That's the reason why, when it's our turn to put on an evening gown, the prospect of the occasion fills most of us with dread and terror!

By definition, an evening gown is a long flowing women's dress worn to a formal event. It ranges from tea and ballerina to floor-length gowns. They are usually made of luxurious fabrics like silk, velvet, satin, organza or chiffon (Wikipedia). Although today's evening gowns come in various silhouettes like straight sheaths, mermaid, A-line or bias cuts, the full-skirted ball gown (think Cinderella) remains the pinnacle of formality.

Here are my tips for evening gown shopping:

1. Shop for the evening gown when you are not desperate. That means, when you pass a sale rack with evening gowns on it, stop to take a look, and if you see anything you like, go ahead and try it; even if you do not have any black-tie function to go to on the horizon.

2. Find an evening gown that flatters your best features. Eg: If you have nice shoulders, go for a strapless gown; if you like your back, find a dress that has a low back feature, if you have amazing legs, choose a gown with high, sexy slits. I propose, accentuating ONE feature, that is to say,

don't find a gown that is strapless and cinched in at the waist and has thigh high slits. Too many accents is a distraction in my books, so go with one or 2 at most and be confident!

3. If you foresee that you will not need to wear evening gowns too often, pick a gown in a fabric that is relatively season-less like silk or chiffon. Also, pick a gown with details that are timeless. Avoid too much beading, sequins, loud prints or ruffles.

4. Choose a darker color that flatters your complexion, or try something in jewel tones. You can always wear different accessories or change your hairstyle and makeup the next time you wear the evening gown.

Embellishments

Embellishments are a quick way to glam up any outfit. In recent years, designers have come up with many creative ideas to embellish virtually anything! Embellishments have also become much fancier with sequins, studs, rhinestones, pearls and crystals in every color palette available. These embellishments can make even a humble tee-shirt worthy of a gala dinner, and a tank top look like body armour!

For everyday style, I suggest pairing an embellished cardigan with a plain top, or wear an embellished tee-shirt with jeans. If that is too much for your taste, try using embellishments as an accent, either on the collar of a shirt, on shoes or a clutch bag. Remember to keep the rest of your outfit and accessories clean and simple thought, you don't want to end up looking like a Christmas tree!

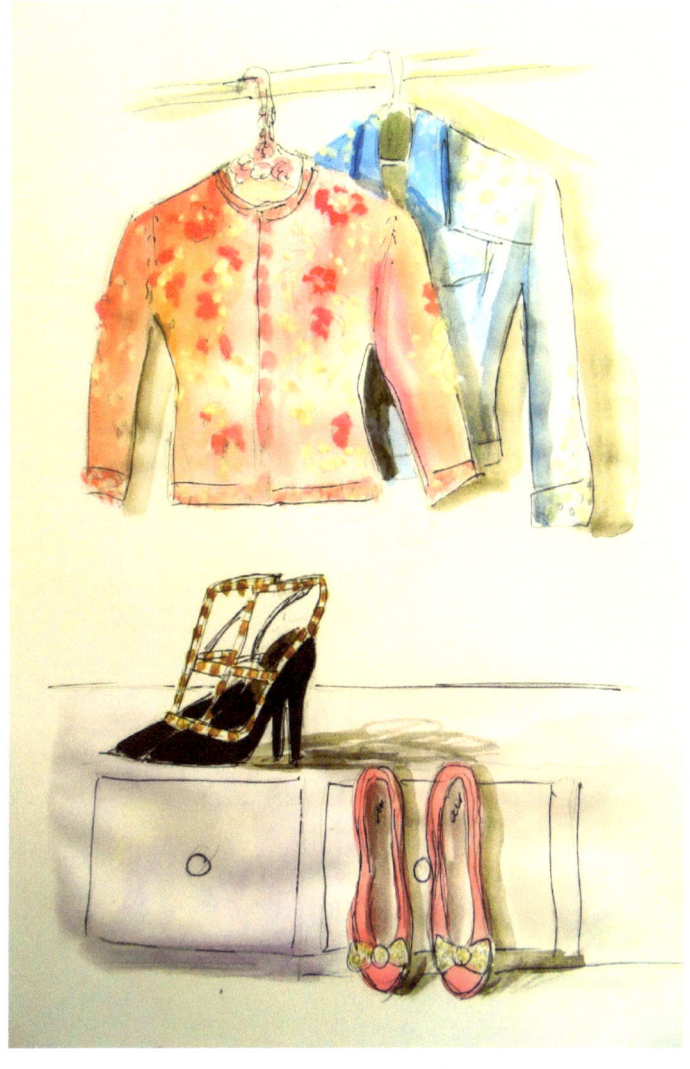

"Fashion is instant language"

Miuccia Prada

Fishnet Stockings

Fishnet stockings are super sexy when done correctly and atrociously awful when done wrong. They had their famous moments when Marlene Dietrich wore them in 1920, the flapper girls wore them in the1930's for those sensational Charleston dances. More recently, Dita Von Teese revitalised them again when she wore them in the movie "Burlesque".

These days, fishnet stockings are commonly worn by the mainstream as a fashion statement, although it still serves some component of sexual fetishism. Technically, fishnet stockings are undergarments that define curves by applying a grid close to the female form, so that it accentuates the wearer's muscular definition.

Here are 3 simple tips to remember when wearing fishnet stockings:

1. Choose a smaller mesh, keep them to less than ½cm squares. They stretch when worn, so tighter and smaller meshes are universally more flattering for all.

2. Don't do grunge, punk or goth with this look unless it's your industry. Fishnet stockings go much better with chic and simple pieces, like a button-down shirt and pencil skirt ensemble.

3. Lastly and most important of all, refrain from pairing mini skirts and towering stilettos with fishnet stockings at ALL costs. Just a peek is all we need to cultivate an air of intrigue. Too much leg showing and the interest and mystery is lost.

Flannel Shirt

Flannel shirts are the coziest of clothing. They are the perfect marriage of comfort and style, something all of us can value and appreciate. They are so easy to throw on over a plain tee shirt and jeans in Spring, or wear under a chunky sweater for Fall. In fact, I think the flannel shirt is a rugged alternative to a classic cardigan.

Flannel is a soft woven fabric, made from carded wool or worsted yarn, although nowadays, it is mainly made from wool, cotton or even synthetic fibers. Carding is a process that breaks up the wool fibers so that they lie sort of parallel to one another. Flannel may also be brushed to create additional softness, or remain un-brushed. It is usually use to make tartan (or plaid) clothing, bed sheets, blankets and sleepwear.

Flannel can be traced back to the 17th century in Wales, where farmers wore flannel shirts to protect themselves from the harsh elements that characterize the region. Somewhere along the way, Scottish plaid got printed on flannel and the 2 were so often used together that one became synonymous with the other until this day. The rise of the grunge look in the 90's with pop bands like Nirvana also fanned the popularity of the flannel shirt, as did the hippy culture from the 70's.

I recommend that you get a flannel shirt with a plaid print and color of your choice. There will be many ways to wear the shirt, and they will always be cosy and stylish, so what's holding you back?

"Give a girl the right shoes, and she can rule the world."

Marilyn Monroe

Graphic Tees

One of the earliest sightings of Graphic Tees must be the 1939 film "The Wizard of Oz". Three men attending to the Scarecrow at the "Wash & Brush-up" Company in Emerald City were seen wearing green T-shirts with the word "Oz" printed on them (Wikipedia).

In the 1950's, the invention of Plastisol (an ink used for screen printing on fabrics) allowed designers more freedom to explore the art of printing logos and slogans on Tee-shirts. Graphic Tees have since been used by music bands, political parties, freedom fighters, and even fashion houses to sell, promote, market and further their various causes through the years. In short, the Graphic Tee became the perfect medium for any person or organisation to express themselves through, art or slogans or swear allegiance to any brand in an inexpensive way.

For me, Graphic Tee-shirts are perfect for lounging around the house or just hanging out with girlfriends on weekends. The key is to find one with a message that speaks to you; resonates with your personality, so to speak. For example, if you wear a band tee-shirt, make sure it's a band you like, with songs you know!

With Graphic Tee, it's perfectly alright to have a silly or fun message. Pair it with a slick pair of jeans so that you don't come across as a groupie! Alternatively, wear it with a full skirt and heels for grown-up girlie charm, or match it with a biker jacket, pencil skirt and ankle booties for a rocker chic style. Add a statement necklace or some arm candy and you're good to go. The possibilities are vast, so go ahead and have fun with it.

Gold

Gold is a chemical element with the symbol Au (from Latin: aurum which means dawn) and atomic number 79. In its purest form, it is a slightly reddish yellow, dense, soft, malleable and ductile metal. Its brightness has survived time, burial and the forces of decay. As early as 1361–1352BC, Egyptian King Tutankhamen and his queen were depicted wearing woven linen embroidered with gold. A sample cloth from the 4th or 5th century BC demonstrates that the ancient Greeks wore gold embroidery. This is evidence that since ancient times, gold has held its place as a precious metal and color, signifying social position, wealth and royalty, while imparting to the wearer glamour and glitz.

In our modern society, gold is no longer restricted to simply precious metal jewelry. In fact, to me gold is a neutral color that goes with everything. You may want to consider expanding your gold vocabulary to include shoes, clutches and even eye shadow. Do not restrict your gold outings solely to dainty gold jewelry, like pendants, chains and rings. Gold studs and rivets are great as embellishments on jackets and t-shirts. If you feel like injecting a bit of drama into your wardrobe, how about getting a gold-sequined top? You can match it with a tulle skirt a la Carrie Bradshaw. If gold is not your color, simply find another metallic shade that you fancy. Choose from an array of colors like silver, rose gold, bronze or pewter. I'm sure you'll be able to find something that works for you.

H

"If honor be your clothing, the suit will last a lifetime; but if clothing be your honor, it will soon be worn threadbare."

William Arnot

Hoop Earrings

There is a hoop earring for everyone. Like the diamond stud earrings, there are very few outfits that cannot be matched with a pair of hoop earrings. My suggestion to keep things classic would be a pair of gold or silver hoops. Personally, I like those that go all the way round and come full circle to clasp at the back of the ears. If you like to glam things up even more, go for a pair of hoops with some pave diamonds. Remember to choose your hoops in proportion to your face, hair and neckline. The general rule is that the larger the hoops, the thinner it should be and the sexier you'll look. Conversely, thicker hoops should be shorter and they will look more classic. Never wear hoops that are thick and long unless you are a part-time gypsy, or attending a fancy dress party as a pirate!

For everyday style, hoop earrings go great with tube dresses because with the décolletage bare, wearing hoop earrings will accentuate the neck. Just make sure that you don't wear any distracting necklaces. Hoop earrings work very well with turtlenecks too, because with everything else covered up, your hoop earrings get all the attention. You may also want to consider tying your hair back into a bun or a ponytail.

If you are already wearing lots of layers; eg: vests, cardigans, jackets, shawls etc, your hoop earrings may not get their chance to shine. In this case, it may be wiser to wear studs instead. Another situation where hoop earrings may not be advisable is at events involving dancing or strenuous sports. For practical reasons, it may be wiser to be light and fuss-free during these events. Wearing huge hoops on your ears may look good for a while, but as time and activities progress, these hoops can get quite heavy. Furthermore, if someone else accidentally pulls on your hoops it would be a mood spoiler for sure.

High-Heeled Shoes

"Give the girl the right shoes and she can conquer the world." (Marilyn Monroe). Few things makes a woman feel sexier and more powerful than wearing a pair of killer stilettos. Those few inches off the ground makes all the difference between dowdy and drama. The walk changes instantly, the hips sway and the personal confidence simply soars. Did you know that centuries ago, it used to be the men who wore the heels? In fact, in the 9th century, Persian horseback warriors wore an extended heel for keeping their feet from sliding out of stirrups. This heel provided balance for the riders when they needed to stand up on horseback and shoot arrows (like today's cowboy boots) (Wikipedia).

Later, high-heeled shoes moved to Europe, where aristocrats embraced the footwear. A painting from 1701 shows King Louis XIV of France, posing regally in a pair of red-heeled shoes, beating Christian Loubotin by 3 centuries (Hyacinthe Rigaud, Portrait of King Louis XIV, 1701, oil on canvas. Musée du Louvre, Paris). In the 16th century, European royalty started wearing high-heeled shoes to make themselves look taller. High-heeled shoes showed the wearer's nobility, authority and wealth, hence the term "well-heeled".

In modern society, high-heeled shoes remain a very important part of women's fashion footwear. High heels force the body to tilt, emphasizing the hips, lengthening the legs, slimming the calves, making the feet look smaller, and forcing the wearer to sway her hips when she walks. Even if science has showed evidence that extended wear of high-heeled shoes can cause foot damage like corns, bunions and hammer toes, most women still consider it a small price to pay in exchange for the surge of feminine power the high-heeled shoes offer.

These days, smart and sexy women do not have to suffer the pain in silence. There are aids that can help alleviate the pain, eg: gel cushions, insoles etc. Be wise and take advantage of these tools; after all, it's impossible to be glamorous when you're limping every step.

My recommendation is that a woman should have at least a pair of black and a pair of nude heels. Throw in a red pair and a bling heel of your choice if you are truly a heels girl. If stilettos are too much for you everyday, vary the heel height, vary skinny and chunky heels for balance. Wedges are a great option to consider too, if you want the height and need the balance.

Here's one shoe-buying exercise worth mentioning: when trying a new pair of stilettos, stand straight with knees straight together and try to tip-toe so that your new heels are at least an inch off the ground. If you cannot create a one inch gap between your heels and the ground, give up those heels. They are angled too high for you to comfortably walk in them for an extended time.

"I like my money right where I can see it.... hanging in my closet."

Carrie Bradshaw

Inspiration and Investment Items

These could mean different things for different people. For some, it could be your investment bag – a Chanel 2.55 or Louis Vuitton Speedy or Hermes Kelly etc. It could be an item that you have saved up for a long time as a significant reward for yourself. It could be a present from a loved one, a family heirloom, an engagement ring, something that puts a smile on your face, and a warm glow in your heart every time you open your wardrobe. Style is not just about putting things together on the outside, but investing and inspiring your inner-self daily. An inspired woman, who is confident of her worth, is a stylish woman indeed!

"Just do it"

Nike

Jeans

Jeans are trousers typically made from denim or dungaree cloth. Research on jeans fabric shows that it emerged from the cities of Genoa, Italy, and Nimes, France. Genes, the French word for Genoa, may be the origin of the word "jeans". In Nimes, weavers tried to reproduce jeans but instead developed a similar twill fabric that became known as denim, from de Nimes, meaning "from Nimes". Genoa's jean was a textile of "medium quality and reasonable cost", very similar to cotton corduroy, and used for work clothes, while Nimes's "denim" was coarser, considered higher quality and used for garments such as smocks and overalls. (Wikipedia).

Whatever the beginnings were, jeans culture has so permeated our urban lifestyle that it has become an undeniable wardrobe staple for every smart woman. So how's a smart woman supposed to shop for jeans? Here are a few practical tips to get you started.

1. Go slow when you shop. Give yourself sufficient time in the fitting room and pick a store with lots of inventory.

2. Make sure you sit or squat while you are trying on jeans in the fitting room. This is to gauge comfort level and also to make sure that not too much butt is showing, especially when you squat down.

3. Do not be fixated about size when fitting on jeans. A size 10 for one brand may fit more like a size 8 or a size 12 in some other brands. When in doubt bring more than 1 size into the fitting rooms. The sales personnel will understand.

4. If budget allows, buy 2 pairs when you find a pair that fits you super well. One pair to hem for heels, and the other to hem for flats. You'll be surprised how fast jean styles get discontinued.

5. Choosing darker denim washes will always make you look slimmer.

6. Bear in mind that special jeans treatments like patches, tears, whiskering, etc. works best for you only if they highlight the areas of your body that you want to accentuate.

7. Decide to have more than 1 pair of jeans from the onset. Wearing one pair of jeans to death reminds me of college days.

8. If you are editing your jeans in your closet, a good rule of thumb is to scan the jeans catalogue of a brand that you admire eg: JCrew, Gap or Levis etc. If the cut of your jeans is no longer available in the current or the last season, it may be time to let your pair of jeans go.

Jewel Tone Colors

Jewel tone colors are derived from the color palette of gemstones eg: ruby, sapphire, amethyst, emeralds, topaz, rose quartz etc. These are rich, saturated and intense colors, and more importantly they are universally flattering for all skin tones.

Jewel tone colors are much more wearable than icy pastels or neon shades. Most of us may not have the courage to don a neon green cocktail dress or be able to carry off a sweet lavender evening gown. But these same garment choices in jewel tones will definitely be deemed stunning and sophisticated.

Wearing the right jewel tone colors close to your face as a dress, blouse, earrings, scarf or necklace, will bring out the color of your eyes and make your skin glow healthily. If your wardrobe is full of neutrals already, try injecting jewel tone pieces into the mix. They are less intimidating, more timeless in the fashion cycle, and much easier to pair with the neutrals that you already own.

"Kindness is always fashionable."

Amelia E. Barr

Khaki Trousers

The name Khaki is a Hindi word that means "dust-colored". From the mid-17th to the 19th century, the British army wore their famous red and white uniforms, which earned the soldiers the name "Red Coats" However, in the mid 1800s, British troops led by Sir Henry Lawrence were sent to guard the Indian frontier. Initially the British Indian troops were dressed in their native costume, which consisted of a kurta and white pajama trousers, subsequently a drab (khaki) uniform was introduced. (Wikipedia).

The khaki pants with their casual look, comfortable fit and durability have held on to their popularity for more than a century! They have remained a stylish wardrobe staple for the upper-class and the preppy. While all khakis are tan in color, the shades of tan vary from light to dark, and the hues can range from grey to brown and green. That said, the neutrality of the khaki color makes it easy to dress up or down.

Khaki is a great neutral for spring/summer as an alternative for white, which is considerably harder to maintain. Khaki pants work best with penny loafers or strappy leather sandals, and pair well with classic-striped, black and white tops. Khaki trousers also match well with black and navy and of course a crisp white button down shirt.

My personal favourite is a khaki and hot-pink combination. Khaki is the ultimate trench coat color (ask Burberry), and Khaki works well with animal print accents too, especially leopard print. If you do not want to add a pair of long khaki trousers to your list of must-buys, consider khaki cropped pants, khaki shorts, or even khaki pencil skirts. As long as you keep the styling utilitarian and simple, khaki is a good all-rounder.

Knits

Simply put, knitting is a technique of producing fabric from a strand of yarn, usually cotton, silk or wool, using one or 2 knitting needles. The earliest record of knitting was found in Egypt circa the 11th century. Before knitting machines were invented, knitting was an arduous task done by hand.

Given our hectic schedules and busy lifestyles, every smart woman should have a few knit pieces in her closet, because knits are virtually crumple-free fashion. Hence, knits make great travelling companions, as they are so easy to pack into a hand carry. Knitted garments are more versatile and comfortable to wear because they are more stretchable than woven fabrics, and mould themselves much better to our bodies.

Every smart woman should have a few different knit cardigans in her wardrobe. Choose from the long and slouchy, cable knit style or a shorter and more fitted look. I'll also suggest a sweater dress, as it goes fantastically well with boots in colder months and ballet flats in summer. Simply find a yarn that is suitable for the climate you live in.

When layering knits, make sure that the piece closest to your body fits you snugly, then choose outer pieces with a loose-cut style. Avoid layering tight on tighter at all costs. You don't want to look like the Michelin man. After washing your knits, lay them flat to dry. This will help to preserve the shape of your knitwear for a longer time.

"Learn from the mistakes of others. You can't live long enough to make them all yourself."

Eleanor Roosevelt

Lace

Lace is an openwork fabric which was probably first created in the early 16th century in Europe. By the late 16th century, noblemen and royalty from England, Spain, Italy and France were all decked in lace! There is a delicate quality in the nature of the fabric, which makes a woman feel very feminine whenever she wears it.

Every smart woman should have a few lace pieces that work for her lifestyle in her wardrobe. Lace is surprisingly versatile and shouldn't be restricted to wedding gowns. I think a simple lace sheath dress in an awesome color is an absolute keeper in anyone's wardrobe.

If all-over-lace is too much for you, consider adding lace accents on a collar, bodice or cuffs, as interesting details for a simple top. How about a colored lace top over a contrast color camisole, or a sexy lace camisole under a sleek tuxedo jacket?

One caution when wearing lace is that you should keep your accessories to the minimum. Lace gets snagged and tears easily. If you feel that white or cream lace is too bridal, try adding colorful accessories to set a cheerful tone. Otherwise, add a biker jacket, a denim jacket or ankle booties to give your lace piece a bit more edge.

Little Black Dress

Before the 1920s, black was a color reserved for mourning. In fact, it was considered indecent to wear black outside such circumstances. However, because of the large number of deaths in World War 1 and the Spanish flu epidemic, it became more common for women to appear in public wearing black. (Wikipedia).

In 1926, Gabrielle "Coco" Chanel, published a picture of a short, simple black dress in American Vogue. Vogue called it "Chanel's Ford". The little black dress was simple and accessible for women of all social classes. Vogue declared that the LBD would become a "uniform for all women of taste". (Wikipedia).

Hollywood's influence on fashion in North America helped the LBD's popularity too, although for much more practical reasons. As Technicolor films became more common, filmmakers relied on these little black dresses because the other colors looked distorted on screen and botched the coloring process! In the 1950s, Hollywood femme fatales were often dressed in sexy LBDs as a contrast to the conservative dresses worn by more wholesome Hollywood stars. (Wikipedia).

Arguably, the most famous LBD of all time was the one Audrey Hepburn wore in the film Breakfast at Tiffany's in 1960. It was designed by Hubert de Givenchy and recently set a record in 2006, when it was auctioned for £410,000 (http://news.bbc.co.uk). This little black dress has certainly stood the test of time!

Audrey Hepburn will endorse my view that the LBD is the ONE MUST HAVE in every stylish woman's wardrobe. Preferably, have 3 or 10! Always remember that the LBD is your blank space. Accessorize it with a great pair of heels, stylish jewelry, sunglasses and a hat even! But make sure they show off your best assets.

Ensure that your LBD is not too tight. Buy it in a good fabric, try to search those with a little stretch or give in the weave of the fabric, since a little stretch goes a long way to help the dress fit better. One last reminder about the beauty of the LBD; it is a blank canvas for YOU, so every time you wear the LBD, make sure you remember to fill up that space confidently and be amazing!

"Minds are like parachutes. They only function when opened."

Thomas Dewar

Man's White Shirt

I love seeing a woman in a man's white shirt. My favourite white shirt fashion moment was when Sharon Stone wore it with a long Vera Wang lavender skirt to the 2006 Academy Awards. Audrey Hepburn wore her white shirt tied around her tiny waist in Roman Holiday and Uma Thurman wore it with black pants in Pulp Fiction. They all looked amazing, yet individually unique!

That, in essence is the beauty of a classic white shirt. It lightens and highlights a person's appearance. It draws attention up to the face, allowing the true beauty and character of the wearer to shine through, and that's why every stylish woman should invest in a nice white shirt. It can be worn at any occasion and is the perfect neutral base, goes with everything and can be dressed up or down.

In fact, in 1992, for the 100th anniversary special of American Vogue, Anna Wintour featured nine supermodels, including Claudia Schiffer, Naomi Campbell, Linda Evangelista, Christy Turlington and Cindy Crawford, on the cover of American Vogue. They all wore the same white shirt from the Gap tied at the waist. It just goes to show that the classic white shirt has stood the test of time and continues to enhance the beauty of the wearer to this day.

Here are a few tips when shopping for a man's white shirt:

1. If you're petite, make sure everything about the shirt is proportionate to your body. Watch out for oversize collars, fussy details, too-long sleeves or too long tails on the shirt.

2. If you're busty, make especially sure that the shirt buttons in the right places so it doesn't gap. Buxom figures should stay away from ruffles or extra details on the upper part of the shirt.

3. For a slimming effect, slightly fitted shirts are better.

4. Check how see-through the shirt is when you try it on.

5. If pure white doesn't enhance your complexion, add a pop of color with a necklace or a scarf.

Finally, simply keep the style of your white shirt as close to a man's version as possible, no fancy buttons or necklines. We're looking for a simple, button down man's white shirt in good-quality cotton. Wear it with sunglasses, red lipstick, skinny jeans, pencil skirt, full skirt, tulle skirt, denim cutoffs, stilettos, sneakers, ballet flats… whatever… and lots of lots of attitude (wink).

Mary Janes

Mary Jane is an American term for a closed, low-cut shoe with one or more straps across the instep. They were originally children's shoes, typically made of black leather or patent leather, with one strap fastened with a button or buckle. Little girls wore them with stockings and that Lolita factor has been attached to these shoes ever since. There's a Renaissance painting of King Henry VIII of England wearing a pair of Mary Janes, displaying evidence that the shoes were previously unisex, and worn by nobility and the elite of society. (Wikipedia). These shoes became popular in the 20's – 30's because the flapper ladies danced in them, and suddenly women everywhere wanted a pair!

Manolo Blanik's Mary Jane moment in "Sex and the City", truly elevated this shoe to urban-fashion-legend status forever. In case you didn't know, the celebrated shoes are a pair of pointy-toed Mary Jane stilettoes, in patent black leather. Otherwise, I suggest you look out for a pair in animal print, or an accent color of your choice and as high a heel as you can dance in! The honest truth is that most women choose Mary Janes because they're practical. The strap across the instep secures the shoes in place, so for women with unequally-sized feet, Mary Janes are a great idea!

Here are a few considerations when shopping for a pair of Mary Janes:

1. If you have wide feet, Mary Janes make your feet look wider because of the horizontal strap across the instep. Hence, if you feel that your feet are exceptionally wide, its probably best to give Mary Janes a miss, or look for those with straps that

run on a diagonal, as diagonal lines have a universally slimming effect.

2. Mary Jane shoes are famed for their Lolita factor (they were originally children's shoes after all), and they can look juvenile even on the most sophisticated of women. To avoid looking like you are five years old, avoid Mary Janes that are too childish in style. By this I mean, avoid flat-soled Mary Janes, and styles with very rounded toes and chunky heels. If you can't avoid wearing these styles, be very mindful about the sophistication level of the rest of your outfit.

3. Look for more grown-up Mary Janes, like high-heeled Mary Janes with pointier toes (like the urban legend shoe). Look for sleeker styles that don't look like they were made for children, funkier pairs that are more edgy than juvenile. Remember to keep your outfits sleek, chic and streamlined whenever you wear your Mary Janes.

"Nobody cares if you can't dance well. Just get up and dance. Great dancers are not great because of their technique, they are great because of their passion."

Martha Graham

Nude

There are lots of ways to do "nude", these days and I don't mean "naked". In fact the nude color palette has become a must-have in a smart woman's wardrobe for very valid reasons. Firstly, nudes are delicate and feminine and offer a refreshing option to black, white and navy. Nudes are subtle and elegant, making the wearer look effortlessly classy.

The key lies in finding the right shade of nude for your complexion. The nude palette ranges from ivory, beige, peach and pinks. Find a shade of nude that is a few shades lighter or darker than your skin tone to avoid looking "naked". Generally, warm-toned ladies look better in beige and peach while cool-toned ladies look better in ivory and pink. (To test if you have warm or cool skin tone: check your veins at your wrist. Green veins means you are warm, blue veins means you are cool.)

Tips for wearing nudes:

1. Always apply slightly more makeup when wearing nude shades, especially if the nude color is close to your face, as in a dress or a top. Put on a brighter blush or a bolder lip color than usual to avoid looking washed out.

2. If you are going to go nude all over, wear separates in slightly different textures and complementary tones of nude so as not to look too monochromatic or washed-out. Lighter and

medium tones of nude together create an interesting color progression that keeps a look fresh and exciting.

3. Nudes pair very well with leopard print because technically, leopard print is brown. Showing a peek of leopard print (whether with a scarf, bag or tights) in a head-to-toe nude outfit is surprising and fun.

4. If head-to-toe nude is too bland for you, try adding black and grey when working with a nude color palette. Black and grey are urban workwear colors, so adding them to nude creates contrast to the outfit instantly.

5. A good way to incorporate nude into your wardrobe is with a pair of nude heels. Nude heels are the perfect work wardrobe staple because they go with everything. In fact, if you had to commit to just one work shoe, the most versatile is not black. It's nude. You can wear your nude pumps with black, grey, brown, colors, more nudes — there are no limits. Nude heels always slim your legs and make you look taller, and now studies show that elevation is power. Nude heels are classic, so invest in a quality pair without trendy details, take care of them properly, and they will serve you well for years.

Necklaces

According to an interesting source (http://visforvintage.net), did you know that a necklace was originally a pagan protective device to stop the soul from leaving the body and flying off without you? Sounds like a pretty essential piece of a smart woman's wardrobe! Trivia aside, I love necklaces because they are a really quick way to dress up your outfit and add a quick signature to your style before you dash out of the house in the morning.

Here are a few fun ways to wear your necklaces:

1. Layer up. A mix of necklaces in varying shapes and lengths can look festive. Add multiple long or short chains together, mixing metals like gold, silver or rose gold. Stop at a few strands though, you don't want to look weighed down.

2. An open neckline on top or a solid color shirt is a great blank canvas for your chunky, colorful necklace to shine. Alternatively, a plain crew neck or a turtle-neck knit top is also great for showing off an awesome necklace. Remember to keep the focus on the statement necklace and keep all other accessories to a minimal.

3. Generally, longer necklaces go with longer dresses and shorter hemlines look more proportionate with shorter necklaces.

4. These days, it doesn't matter if the stones on the necklaces are real or fake, dainty or chunky,

single or layered. The more important consideration is the vibe you are going for. Eg: Adding multiple strands of ful beads will give a bohemian or hippy style, wearing chunky silver chains will feel more punk or metal, wearing pearls gives a classy appearance and wearing chunky gold chains may invoke a rapper image! Make sure the necklaces tell your style story accurately, that's all I'm saying.

"One of the best things that ever happened to me is that I'm a woman.

That's the way all females should feel."

Marilyn Monroe

Opaque Tights

Opaque tights are a life-saver and a must-have for every smart women's wardrobe because they cover a multitude of imperfections on our legs and give us the freedom to look sexy, not scandalous. Some even have control tops, to help us hold in our bellies and bums, shaping our legs to look leaner and slimmer. My personal recommendation is to choose tights that are matt and perfectly opaque, without shine and not sheer.

Here are a few tips to remember when wearing or shopping for tights:

1. Opaque tights are not pants. Do not EVER wear them out on their own.
2. Do not wear nude or flesh-colored opaque tights. These are very aging and do not flatter your legs. While we're at it, I wouldn't wear green tights either as they bring back memories of Peter Pan.
3. If you want extra long legs, keep the skirt, tights and heels in the same color, preferably black for maximum slimming effect.
4. Never wear tights with sandals or slippers.
5. Don't wear socks over tights unless you are a teenager.
6. Never show your reinforced toes of tights in shoes.

7. When in doubt, buy good-quality, matt, black opaque tights. They are universally slimming for everybody.

I learnt this great tip from eBay to extend the life of tights. Begin by buying tights that are at least 15 percent Lycra or spandex, because such tights will hold up the best. To keep them looking great and run-free, freeze them. Run tights under water, wring them out and place them in a freezer bag in the freezer for 24 hours. Freezing tights will strengthen the fibres. After 24 hours, let the tights thaw out naturally. The tights will be stronger and their lifespan will be extended from a few months to closer to a year.

"Pay no attention to what the critics say... Remember a statue has never been set up in honour of a critic."

Jean Sibelius

Pencil Skirt

The pencil skirt is arguably a woman's best weapon in the boardroom. It asserts a powerful feminine vibe while conjuring images of femme fatale vulnerability at the same time. Simply put, it's downright sexy! A smart woman in a pencil skirt, wearing the highest pair of heels she can walk in, is a force to be reckoned with in the boardroom indeed. You can bet your bottom dollar (no pun intended), she knows exactly what she's doing.

Here are a few helpful tips for nailing the perfect pencil skirt:

1. It should be snug but never too tight.
2. It should end just above or just below the knees.
3. Always wear it with high heels. Flats will not do. Period.
4. Look for a pencil skirt with some stretch in the fabric. This will give you smoother shape definition without being too tight or gaping at the wrong places.
5. A slit at the side or back of the pencil skirt will make it easier for you to walk in and it's immeasurably much more sexy to watch, too.
6. Try a high waisted pencil skirt and belt it well, to emphasize the hourglass figure for added effect.

Pearls

Pearls have long been a symbol of wealth and status. They have never gone out of fashion with the rich and the elite of society. Whether the pearls were cultured, real or fake was immaterial. The reputation of this gemstone has fascinated us for centuries. Long layers of pearls were Coco Chanel's trademark accessory, while Jackie O was known for her triple strands of short, cultured pearls.

The best advice I've heard about pearls is to not take them too seriously. The other is to wear only one pearl accessory at one time. Don't do the pearl earrings, pearl rings plus pearl necklace all in one outfit, unless you are the sales promoter at a pearl wholesaler! Instead, try layering pearl necklaces of different lengths with other chain necklaces for added effect. Pearls are incredibly versatile. They match equally well with a little black dress, an evening gown or jeans and a plain tee-shirt.

Depending on your budget, you can buy the real stuff at Mikimoto (best retailer of cultured pearls in my opinion) or buy gorgeous South Sea Pearls in a variety of colors, from gold to peacock green, grey or cream, from any reputable jeweler. You can also check out eBay or scour vintage shops for vintage pearl necklaces with a bit of history. Or buy baroque pearls, which are irregularly shaped naturally, and come in a myriad of colors too! As with all accessories, pick the one that speaks to you, and then wear it with loads of attitude.

"Quality is remembered long after the price is forgotten."

Gucci Slogan

Quirky Prints

Every smart woman needs to have a few items with quirky prints in her wardrobe. These can be tops, skirts, dresses, scarves or even shoes. These quirky prints should give glimpses of your style personality and make you smile whenever you see them or put them on.

Here are a few tips when shopping for prints:

1. Keep the silhouettes and shapes of the printed clothing simple; that way, it will be easier to pair them with the staples you already have in your wardrobe.

2. The idea is for the quirky print to stand out, so avoid fussy details like ruffles, complicated cuts, stitching etc. Choose smooth rather than textured fabrics for the same reason.

3. Be mindful of the scale of the print in proportion to your size. A tiny all-over print on a larger woman never works out, a large and bold print on a petite woman completely overwhelms her as well. As a general guide, do not buy an all-over print that is larger than your clenched fist.

4. If you are a print novice, start with a monochrome print in a color family that you are comfortable with, eg a black shirt with white cats printed all-over, or a navy pencil skirt with white polka dots.

5. To avoid looking too kitschy, keep to one print per outfit and keep the rest of the outfit, including accessories, simple and minimal.

Quilted Jackets

Quilting became popular in the 17th century, although its roots can be traced back to the middle ages. In the beginning, quilting was mainly used for bed covers. Technically speaking, quilting refers to any run of stitching – decoratively or in a straight run – that combines at least two layers of cloth together to make a thicker padded material. Often, a third padding layer or interlining between the cloth is added, providing the three dimensional look on diamond quilted jackets. The term 'quilt' seems to have originated in England in the 12th century, and is derived from the Latin word cucita, which means cushion or bolster. (Wikipedia).

There's something rather comforting about wearing a quilted jacket. Perhaps it has something to do with its history as a source of padding for armour. There was a medieval padded jacket called a gambeson. If you were rich, you wore it under your armour to prevent chafing. If you were poor, you wore it on its own and, presumably, died fairly quickly in the battlefield!

The quilted jacket is a very practical item of clothing to have in a smart woman's wardrobe when the outdoor temperatures start to plunge. It is lightweight and insulating and these days, most quilted jackets come with a water resistant shell. Scientifically, the layers of the quilted jacket trap air, which acts as an insulator, and the quilt stitching keeps the insulating materials such as down feathers or polyester fibres from moving around.

Quilted jackets are perfect as travelling companions to cold countries because unlike those huge and heavy woolen coats, quilted jackets can be easily compressed into a small handcarry or luggage. When summer arrives, quilted jackets can be vacuum-sealed and packed away, giving you space in your wardrobe.

Shopping tips for a quilted jacket:

1. Know your purpose for the quilted jacket. Pick one in a neutral color to get more city wear out of it , or pick a bright color if you intend to do outdoor sports like hiking or skiing (for safety reasons), in a fleece density suitable for the weather.

2. I prefer goose down feathers rather than polyester fibers, simply because goose down is natural fibre and warmer, but I think you can find some good-quality quilted jackets with polyester fibers too.

3. Bear in mind that quilted jackets are hard to alter so ensure that they fit you well, especially sleeves and body length.

4. For practical reasons, pick a quilted jacket with a water-resistant or water-proof outer shell and a removable hoodie. If it's a slight drizzle, you can still get around town with a hoodie quilted jacket, no need for an umbrella.

5. Do not buy a too tight quilted jacket. Bear in mind that you will probably wear layers under this jacket, so give yourself some space. We don't want to look like the Michelin man, ever!

"Remember this: No one is looking at your imperfections; they're all too busy worrying about their own."

Isaac Mizrahi

Red Lipstick

Red lipstick is a non-negotiable for a smart woman's wardrobe. It's like your little black dress or your man's white shirt and your favourite blue jeans. You have to find the best red lipstick for YOU. Any cosmetic brand worth its weight will have a range of red lipsticks, so take your time to find the "ONE" that is best for you. There is no one RED that fits all; it depends on your eye, hair and skin color.

When wearing red lipstick, keep the rest of your makeup and even accessories minimal. Let your lips take centre stage as nothing beats the power of red lips. A crimson pout will raise your game, up your sex factor and make a statement, all in one swipe!

Here are my tips for wearing red lipstick:

1. Simply wear red lipgloss and nothing else, if you prefer the "barely there" feel.

2. The "proper" way to wear red lipstick for daytime is to apply concealer all round the lips, blotting it before applying red lipstick to avoid smudges. Kiss a tissue paper with your newly applied lipstick, then apply a second coat of red lipstick for a more even application that will last throughout the day.

3. For evening glamour, line your lips with red lip pencil, then re-apply your red lipstick for the whole glamorous diva look.

4. If your lips are thin, avoid deep reds as they will make your lips look even thinner than they already are.

5. To avoid getting teeth stained by lipstick, after application, put your finger in your mouth, purse your lips around your finger, then pull it out slowly to remove any excess color of the lipstick and you're good to go.

Rompers

Rompers first appeared in USA in the early 1900s as a one piece garment worn by younger children. People thought they were ideal for movement, therefore great for kids as a playsuit. These days, rompers have become a summer staple because they are incredibly easy to wear and require very little maintenance. Think of the romper as the short version of the jumpsuit, another very versatile piece for a smart woman's wardrobe.

Here are my favourite tips for styling a romper:

1. Rompers usually come with an elastic waist to make them easier to wear. I'm not a fan of elastic waists, although I understand the practicalities of it. I feel that adding a nice belt will hide the elastic waist and personalize your outfit at the same time.

2. Rompers are essentially a one-piece shorts and top set. They tend to make the wearer look cute, youthful and casual. To present a more polished

look, simple throw a nice blazer over the romper for a dash of class.

3. Depending on the weather, you can wear rompers with tights, boots and motorcycle jacket for autumn/winter or bare legs and sandals in the summer!

4. Finally, a gentle word of caution. Please bear in mind that rompers should be worn loose and comfy. Do not wear a romper that is too tight, you do not want to look like Catwoman!

"Style is knowing who you are, what you want to say and not giving a damn."

Orson Welles

Sunglasses

History records that the Roman Emperor Nero liked to watch gladiator fights with emerald glasses. Sunglasses made from flat panes of smoky quartz which protected the eyes from glare were used in China as early as the 12th century. Ancient documents record that Chinese judges wore crystal sunglasses in their courts to conceal their facial expressions while questioning witnesses. (Wikipedia).

These days, celebrities all over the world still wear sunglasses to hide their expressions and disguise their appearances from the public. Of course, these days, sunglasses do more than just cut the glare from the sun. When shopping for sunglasses, look out for sunglasses that look fabulous on you AND are safe for your eyes. Choose to wear sunglasses that offer 100% UV protection. It is proven that wearing proper sunglasses reduces the risk of eye damage due to sun exposure. My sincere advice is to never buy cheap fashion glasses from street vendors or replicas, no matter how fashionable they look. Your eyes are worth much more than these.

Argueably, the 3 most famous sunglasses styles are. 1. The Aviator (worn by Tom Cruise in Top Gun and Kate Hudson in Almost Famous), 2. The Wayfarer (worn by Audrey Hepburn in Breakfast at Tiffany's, Emma Watson, Reese Witherspoon and Emily Brunt) and 3. Nina Ricci 3203 (worn by Jackie Kennedy, and Nicole Richie). These shapes have stood the test of time, so if you want a classic pair, try them out and choose the one that is best for your face shape!

Suit

Every woman in the professional arena should own at least one matching suit. If you can own two suits, then get one in a solid neutral color (read black, navy, grey, dark brown, beige), and one a timeless texture (like tweed) or print (like hounds tooth or stripes). This will allow you room for mixing and matching, eg solid jacket with tweed skirt or tweed jacket with solid-colored trousers.

When it comes to suits, do not compromise on FIT. A suit MUST fit you – Perfectly, period. If it doesn't, get it tailored. Do not accept slouchy shoulders, trousers with hems sweeping the floor or too long sleeves. It never works, it never will. The message of a suit is sleek sophistication. You want to look sharp and smart and be taken seriously. Frumpy is not an option.

I'm partial to an immaculate, solid black suit. Wear it with stilettoes and a plain white camisole or a button-down crisp white shirt. You can also wear a lace tank top under your suit for some contrasting textures. If you are brave and your work environment is agreeable, just wear the suit with nothing underneath.

When dressed in a suit, always keep your makeup simple, wear nude or red lips, add your favourite jewelry and strut your style. A full black suit is very somber and formal, so be aware of the presence it commands.

Wherever possible, try to break up your suit. Wear the jacket with a plain white tee or a graphic tee and jeans. Wear your skirt with a peplum top or a quirky printed blouse. If it's a pair of pants, then match it with a silk blouse or a cardigan. Always, always, always personalize your suits.

"The beauty of a woman is not in the clothes she wears, the figure that she carries, or the way she combs her hair. The beauty of a woman is seen in her eyes, because that is the doorway to her heart, the place where love resides. True beauty in a woman is reflected in her soul. It's the caring that she lovingly gives, the passion that she shows & the beauty of a woman only grows with passing years."

Audrey Hepburn

T-Shirt

T-shirt is to clothes what hot chocolate is to comfort food. They started out as men's undergarments and were made out of light, inexpensive and easy-to-clean fabrics. The earliest T-shirt record dates back to the Spanish-American War in 1913, when the U.S. Navy issued them as undergarments for U.S. Navy soldiers. Following World War II, it became common to see veterans wearing their uniform trousers with their T-shirts as casual clothing. In 1951, after Marlon Brando wore a T-shirt in A Street Car Named Desire, the humble T-shirt finally achieved its status as a stand-alone fashion item. (Wikipedia).

Since then, the humble T-shirt has become a worldwide unisex wardrobe staple. It has also become a medium for self-expression and advertising, with any imaginable combination of words, art and photographs on display. (Wikipedia). The all-time classic for me is still a Hanes cotton T-shirt, crew neck and short-sleeves, with a tubular knitted body; although these days, T-shirt manufacturers are constantly improving their technology to make the perfect T-shirt.

Every smart woman's wardrobe should have a stack of t-shirts in basic and a few of her favourite colors. Look for cotton T-shirts with some stretch or lycra in them, for better fit and comfort. Buy better-quality T-shirts that will not loose their shape easily after washing. Lay your T-shirts flat to dry, so that they will not lengthen while drying. Generally, T-shirts keep their shape better if you store them folded in a chest of drawers. Be ruthless when editing your old T-shirts. If there are holes, tears, discolorations, wonky necklines etc, it's time to let them go. You should replace your t-shirts every 3-6 months, depending on the frequency you wear them.

Tuxedo

The tuxedo is sometimes referred to as a "smoking suit" as per its English origins. In 1966, French designer Yves Saint Laurent sent his models on the runway in tuxedo jackets and women everywhere fell in love with the tuxedo and embraced it into their wardrobes.

Here are 3 simple tips for wearing a tuxedo:

1. Like any suit, it should flatter your womanly silhouette and fit you perfectly.
2. Wear a lace camisole underneath or if you're feeling bold, don't wear anything underneath. Its super sexy and classy.
3. Wear the highest stilettoes you can manage with a full tuxedo suit. You may even want to add a vintage brooch or corsage on the lapel, just for some added personality and pop of fun.
4. This formula is always true.
   Red lips + Black tuxedo = SEXY

"Unless you try to do something beyond what you have already mastered, you will never grow."

Ralph Waldo Emerson

Underwear

Women have been wearing underwear since the Egyptian civilizations. Every smart women knows that the right underwear can make or break an outfit. Wearing great underwear makes you feel sexy immediately. The VPL (visible panty line) is an unforgivable style crime.

Wear your right size. If you don't know your size, please get yourself fitted by a lingerie expert in a mall. If you need a little more control and support to hold in your wobbly bits, I highly recommend shapewear. Try brands like Spanx, Marks & Spencers or Wacoal; they are well-known for the effectiveness and quality of their shapewear.

Visible brassiere straps are not sexy. If the blouse you are wearing has shoulder straps that are too thin, it may be a better option to wear a strapless brassiere, than one with regular straps and risk exposure. Always remember that "what you wear should not be a source of pain, vast expense or misery".

Here are some of my favourite tips when shopping for underwear:

1. Don't confuse fashion and comfort. Underwear sits on your skin all day. Choose comfort over fashion, although these days, one can expect both fashion and comfort to converge at some level.
2. Choose the right size.

3. Look for quality fabric. Fabric can be a big source of discomfort when wearing underwear, especially when its scratchy (like some lace can be), sweat inducing or doesn't breathe. Look for soft fabrics like cotton, lycra, microfiber, bamboo, polyester. Try to get panties with cotton crotches.
4. Consider seamless panties. Seamless underwear makes your clothing look smoother from the outside.

Umbrella

Here's another controversial item in my list of a smart woman's wardrobe – an umbrella. I'm taking a page from the boy scouts motto: "Always be prepared!"

There have been occasions when I trusted the weatherman's prediction that skies would be bright and sunny and then hours later, I'm caught in a surprise downpour and stuck in some unglamorous shelter while waiting for the showers to pass. It's really hard to look stylish when you are drenched wet from head to toe! A stylish woman shouldn't be caught off guard. Why not pack a mini umbrella in your bag everyday to avoid these moments?

If you have to leave the house whilst it is raining, I think it's uber-stylish to bring a sleek, long automatic umbrella and put on your wellies. Think Gene Kelly, singing in the rain….and suddenly your mood is lifted and you're definitely smiling and stylish!

"Virtue and genuine graces in themselves, speak what no words can utter."

William Shakespeare

Voluminous Skirt

The voluminous skirt is a great alternative to the pencil skirt. It fits at the waist and flares out with volume, either from pleats or gathers. For women who are conscious of their hips and thighs, the voluminous skirt is great for hiding imperfections while allowing maximum ease of movement. A voluminous skirt cinches at the waist and emphasizes the hourglass figure. Because of the voluminous nature of the skirt, by contrast, it makes our legs appear slimmer.

If you are concerned that you do not have a flat tummy, find a skirt with large pleats instead of gathers. On the other hand, if your concern is that you have a boyish figure and not enough curves, select a skirt with lots of gathers. Be mindful of the length of the skirt and make sure it is proportional to your height. Generally, taller girls carry longer, midi lengths better. The most flattering length is about 2cm above or below the knees. Since the skirt will make a statement, given its sheer volume, keep the rest of the outfit slim and simple. Stay away from fussy details, or bulky gathers and ruffles on top.

Whichever option you decide, go with a solid color you like; or try a nice print for a more feminine feel. Match the skirts with cropped tops, or tuck a tulle version into a button-down denim shirt for a play of textures and contrasts. Use a belt to accent the cinched-in waist and you're good to go!

Vintage

Adding vintage items into your wardrobe is a really clever way of asserting your personality and differentiating yourself from everybody else. An item is considered VINTAGE if it's made after 1920's and has been around for more than 30 years. Anything made before 1920's that still exists today is ANTIQUE.

When shopping for vintage clothes, be prepared to do your own research beforehand. Read up about fashion history so that you know the popular styles of that era. When vintage shopping, be aware that the clothes have been worn before. That said, be very strict when it comes to quality control. The condition of the garment should be almost new. Do not accept tears, stains or discolorations. If the vintage garment does not fit you make sure that you can take it to your tailor, and that there is sufficient room for her to take it in to your size.

If you are looking for designer vintage, I highly recommend Missoni, Pucci, Valentino and Diane Von Furstenburg. Of course, finding an Yves Saint Laurent tuxedo jacket will be striking a jackpot. If you haven't done vintage shopping before but you are game to try, start out with accessories. Try looking for costume jewelry like earrings, necklaces or brooches, or even belts, bags and clutches. These will definitely be one-of-a-kind conversational pieces that have already stood the test of time.

"We are all the artists of our own lives and we can use as many colors and brushstrokes as we like."

Oprah Winfrey

Watch

Some sources believe that the world's first wristwatch was created by Abraham-Louis Breguet for Caroline Murat, Queen of Naples, in 1810. Wristwatches used to be exclusively worn by women, while men used pocket watches up until the early 20th century. In fact, military men only started to wear wristwatches towards the end of the 19th century, when the importance of synchronizing maneuvers during war was increasingly recognized. (Wikipedia).

Even if you are not into fashion accessories, think of wearing watches as putting on a functional item. See watches as practical timepieces that you can use to reflect your style. Pick one that works with your personality, your budget and your lifestyle.

Here are a few styles options you can consider:

1. Opt for a man's watch and wear it on your slender wrist. We're going for contrast and a cool androgynous style.

2. Go for a true-blue vintage wind-up timepiece. Do your homework, find a reputable second-hand watch shop, and invest in a watchmakers watch. Every time you wear it, you'll be wearing a piece of history on your wrist.

3. Get a dainty, feminine bracelet watch like those Elizabethan women of the 19th century use to wear.

4. Invest in a diamond encrusted luxury timepiece that doubles up as a piece of jewelry. A word of caution, if you are going to burn some cash, make sure it's a watchmaker's watch with an international warranty.
5. Get a classic watch with a leather strap and a clean face. It goes with everything in your wardrobe.
6. Find a swatch with a colorful plastic strap that's always fun to wear. There are lots of colors and prints to choose from.
7. Be a techno geek. Get a watch that tells time, counts the calories you burn, measures your blood pressure, the number of hours you sleep, allows you to check your email messages and is a mobile device all at the same time!

Whatever your fancy, there is a watch that suits your needs perfectly.

Wrap Dress

A smart woman must have a wrap dress in her wardrobe, preferably in a jersey knit. Look for one in silk jersey or in a viscose jersey knit. It's a no-brainer for travels; it's great for the boardroom, and versatile enough for after-dinner drinks with the gals.

The wrap dress was created by Diane Von Furstenburg in 1974 and it launched a liberating style movement for women around the globe. By 1976, Diane

Von Furstenburg had sold over a million of her signature dresses and landed on the cover of "The Wall Street Journal" and "Newsweek", dubbing her 'the most marketable woman since Coco Chanel'. (http://www.dvf.com)

The popularity of this same wrap dress has lasted till today and shows no signs of waning. This is because this dress flatters the feminine form perfectly. The V-neckline accentuates the cleavage and lengthens the neck, the wrap-around ties cinches the waist in for an hourglass figure. What else can a woman ask for?

Get one in a solid color or in a monochrome print. You'll probably get more wear out of it if you picked one in neutral color palette. If for whatever reason you are fortunate enough to chance upon a vintage DVF wrap dress from the 1970s in your size, grab it with both hands and never let it slip by!

Wedges

Wedges are my all-time favourite shoe. They provide the height of stilettoes, the stability of flats, and they look much nicer than platforms! Wedge heels are sturdier and more comfortable than the typical high heel, they create an illusion of longer legs and thinner ankles while providing better support at the arch of the foot.

The wedge heel was invented by Mr Salvatore Ferragamo in the 1930s. It had a triangular heel or wedge-like piece that runs from the front of the foot to the back, rather than sitting just under the heel. Due to the war, there was a shortage of leather and rubber and Mr Ferragamo began experimenting with non-tradition materials such as cork and wood.

The wedge heel with cork platform became the most popular because of its lightness and durability. Women found the wedge heel easier to walk in, and applauded its support of the foot and the comfort it afforded in walking. Within 2 years of its introduction to the world of fashion, the wedge heel became a classic and its popularity remains to this day.

Here are my key considerations for buying wedges:

1. The chunky wedge heel looks better on women with slightly thicker ankles and muscular calves. In fact, for women with slender ankles and slimmer calves, wearing wedge heels may cause your feet and calves to look even thinner than they actually are.

2. The height of the wedges you pick depends on your threshold of pain. Low 1"-2" sandals wedges are super comfortable and perfect for casual outfits, like a simple t-shirt and shorts / jeans combination. My favourite wedge heel height is 2"- 2 ½". They give the right amount of heel and visually lengthen your legs, at this height they are also comfortable enough to go shopping in, for walks in the park etc. 3"- 4" heels are chic and sassy, but may not be the most comfortable height for most occasions. Going higher than 4" is best kept for special occasions.

3. Pick wedges with minimal details and versatile styles like espadrilles, peep toes and closed pump wedges, so that they will match well with most of

the outfits in your wardrobe and last for more than one season.

4. Decide on color. You can go with neutrals like nude (highly recommended), black, navy or tan or you can opt to go with a fresh pop of color like red, pink, blue; any color you fancy really...Just remember that colored footwear attracts attention to your feet, so make sure you keep up with your pedicures and shave your legs!

"eXperience: A comb life gives you after you lose your hair."

Judith Stern

X-Factor 1

I have searched long and hard for something essential to include in a smart woman's wardrobe that starts with "X" and the best response I can come up with is "The X-Factor". The X-Factor is defined as an indescribable quality, something about someone that you cannot put your finger on; the French say it best as "je ne sais quoi". In English, it blandly means "I don't know what" but in French, "je ne sais quoi" describes an elusive and pleasing quality that charms.

The effectiveness of a smart woman's wardrobe is more than the sum of its parts. The magic is in the many combinations that these individual items make available simply by their presence in your wardrobe. They are your tools to display various aspects of your personality to the world everyday. Put on a Man's White Shirt with a Voluminous skirt, cinch it at the waist with a Vintage Belt, wear your favourite High Heels and you're out the door feeling stylish in 10 minutes flat. Alternatively, sling a Cardigan over a Graphic tee, match them with your favourite Jeans and Ballet flats and off you go. The combinations these A – Z items afford are endless and I know it sounds cliché, but the power is within you. Your personal style essence is the "X-factor", so have fun with it.

X-Factor 2

There's another angle I want to go at with the "X-Factor" and it's the "multiplication factor". In school, the letter "X" apart from "marking the spot" also stands for multiplication. The A-Z items suggested in this book for a smart woman's wardrobe can be multiplied in whatever quantities that suit your lifestyle needs. If you are a jeans and tee shirt gal, go ahead and get 5 pairs of jeans and 10 tee shirts; if you adore pencil skirts then stock up 3 different colors when you find one with a great fit. There is no shame in repeatedly wearing the same item if you feel fantastic in it and it serves your lifestyle needs. In fact, sometimes a certain consistency builds style confidence; think Jackie O in her sheath dresses and pearls.

"Your journey begins with a choice to get up, step out and live fully."

Oprah Winfrey

Yoga Wear

Every smart woman knows that some form of exercise routine is essential to keep our bodies fit and healthy. It doesn't have to be Yoga, simply find an activity you like and get started. The more stressful our lives are, the more important it is to exercise and keep strong.

So here are my suggestions when shopping for exercise gear:

1. These days, most sportwear companies offer exercise wear made from a synthetic fiber called Polypropylene. Invest in these as they will allow your skin to breathe by drawing sweat away from your body. This will keep you cool while you exercise. Also make sure that your workout clothes have some lycra or spandex in them as these will mould and stretch along with your body as you exercise. There are some lines of workout clothing can even help you manage your body temperature. They may be more expensive but they'll keep you comfortable while you're sweating it out at the gym and they'll probably last longer than your regular gym tees.

2. If you anticipate that you will be sweating a lot, do not wear cotton. Cotton is a breathable, natural fiber and it's a great choice for gentle workouts like walking or stretching, given that it's soft and comfortable. However, when you're doing high-impact or more intense aerobic

exercises and perspiring buckets, your regular cotton tee will soak up all that perspiration, become very heavy, and cling to your body, thereby weighing you down and interfering with your workout. That's why cotton is not a good choice for more intense exercises.

3. Another tip is to avoid any rough fabrics that could chafe or irritate your skin during repetitive movements, instead, select exercise wear that will give you freedom of movement, and not constrict you. In particular, look out for clothes that have a small percentage of spandex, say 5-10%, listed on the label. The spandex will allow for a greater range of motion during exercise while providing a comfortable fit without being skin-tight.

4. Make sure that you include supportive underwear into your exercise wardrobe. A good sports bra is a top priority as it offers you proper support and flexibility while you go through your exercise routines.

5. Tailor your attire to the specific activity. Baggy pants shouldn't be worn for cycling or spinning, just as long and flowing tops won't cover you properly when you do downward dog in yoga class. Think about the activities you do most often, then ensure that the exercise gear you purchase are appropriate for those activities. Generally, a pair of 3/4 workout Capri pants and a dri-fit top will work for most activities, but go

ahead and try on the workout clothes before you buy - and while you're at it, do a few of your workout moves in the dressing room just to be sure that you'll be comfortable in them.

6. Choose exercise clothes that you like, rather than hiding your body under baggy layers. You will feel more confident of yourself when you wear exercise clothes that make you look good. Then, if you feel good about yourself, you'll be more motivated to last throughout the workout and exercise more often.

7. Always remember to wear proper footwear. It is essential to choose a workout shoe that will protect your feet and boosts your performance, regardless of your choice of sports or exercise. Make sure you wear a comfortable athletic shoe that supports your feet and ankles and wear socks if you are inclined to sweaty feet.

These days, sportwear manufacturers have incorporated lots of cool technology into exercise wear. There are anti-microbial treatments to combat odor, built-in ultra-violet protection on clothes to fight the sun's harmful rays, and even luminescent jackets and running gear for those of us that want to exercise when it's dark!

Wearing the right exercise clothes can be the difference between an enjoyable workout and an hour of misery. Perhaps investing in some stylish and comfortable workout gear is the motivation you need to get started. The more often you workout, the more essential it is to wear the right clothes. Good workout wear keeps you comfortable, dry and cool. It can boost your ego while you sweat it out at the gym, so why not put in some effort to find workout wear that flatter your figure so that you can exercise anywhere in style.

"Zest is the secret of all beauty. There is no beauty that is attractive without zest."

Christian Dior

Zippered Hoodies

Hoodies have been part of men's and women's wear for centuries. The word "hood" actually comes from the Anglo-Saxon word "hod", which can be traced back to robes with hoods attached, worn by monks in 12th century England. The hooded sweatshirt was first produced in the USA in the 1930s and sold to laborers working in freezing temperatures in New York.

By the 1970s, the Hip Hop culture and the success of movie "Rocky", contributed to the popularity of the zippered hoodie. The appeal of instant anonymity, provided by the accessible hood, attracted both celebrities and those with criminal intent to the zippered hoodie. Zippered hoodies have since evolved and moved beyond college sweatshirt styles and gym wear into the fashion arena.

My guess is that celebrities all over the world own dozens of these because they are the easiest alternative to put on with sunglasses for a quick run to the grocery store around the corner or to get the Saturday morning coffee. Zippered hoodies are also practical for travel and trips to the gym when the weather turns chilly.

Here are my zippered hoodie shopping tips:

1. Look for a hoodie that is more fitted and sleek. Do not get one in a shiny fabric or a baggy cut unless you are a rapper! You want to look sporty and chic, not sloppy or, worse, frumpy.

2. Do look out for the right length. Never buy a hoodie that ends at the widest part of the hips. The best length is one that ends about halfway down the fly of your jeans; too short, you risk exposing your belly when you raise your hands, too long, it makes you look sloppy.

3. To style a modern hoodie well, get a zippered hoodie in a neutral that works for you. Unless you are a teenager or still in college, stay away from slogans and prints. They will make it look too cutesy or immature.

4. Get one with a thicker, fleeced under-layer or get one in a lighter cotton knit, depending on the temperature of the area you live in.

5. If it's a messy hair day, simply pull up the hood, throw on the sunglasses and you'll look effortlessly mysterious and stylish too!

Parting Words

I hope you enjoyed reading this book! If there's a final thought I'd like to leave you with it's this; don't take this all too seriously. Style is about being comfortable in your own skin while enjoying the varying nuances of fashion, without becoming a fashion victim.

I love the dynamic evolution of fashion, its never-static pulsating pace, with a vibrant life of its own. On the other hand, I love the fact that as individuals, we are in control of our own style language. We have the power and the liberty to decide what goes into our wardrobe and how we want to put the pieces together everyday.

The pieces I have shared in this book are my suggestions of time-tested items a smart and stylish woman should have in her wardrobe. A smart woman knows that at the end of the day, she needs to know how to respect herself enough, to present her authentic self to the world at all times, for herself; not just from Monday to Friday to impress other people. Self confidence is a stunning language.

In conclusion, I like to share one of my favourite quotes of all time by Marianne Williamson from her book Return to Love:

Our deepest fear is not that we are inadequate. Our deepest fear is that we are powerful beyond measure. It is our light, not our darkness that most frightens us.

We ask ourselves, who am I to be brilliant, gorgeous, talented, fabulous? Actually, who are you not to be? You are a child of God. Your playing small does not serve the world. There is nothing enlightened about shrinking so that other people won't feel insecure around you. We are all meant to shine, as children do.

We were born to make manifest the glory of God that is within us. It's not just in some of us; it's in everyone. And as we let our own light shine, we unconsciously give other people permission to do the same. As we are liberated from our own fear, our presence automatically liberates others.

The truth is that the world does watch and react to how you dress yourself everyday. Your ensemble can open doors and create opportunities that may lead to dazzling and joyful journeys. Don't let yourself and the world down by not living up to your own style standards. Only one life, why not live it with grace, gladness and style.

XXX elsie

Acknowledgements

Writing this book would not have been possible if not for the love and encouragement of family, friends & colleagues who believed in my dream of writing a book to make style accessible to every woman.

A million "thank yous" to everyone who has helped me by sharing your precious knowledge, experiences, time and effort to launch this book. I would never get here if not for you.

My deepest appreciation to Ros for your gorgeous illustrations. Your drawings bring my text to life and give beautiful form to my thoughts.

Many thanks to my wonderful family, for believing in me and telling me your honest opinions at all times, even if it meant that I would have to rewrite and miss cooking dinner yet again!

Many thanks to all the awesome gals at Butterflies & Marigolds, for your support and understanding. Thanks for looking after the shops and giving me peace of mind while I write. I'm sorry for the times I could not be at the shops because the book needs tweaking.

My sincere thanks to everyone who bought this book, either for yourself or as a gift, your purchase and support makes my writing possible.

Sources

- Wikipedia: a fantastic source of all sorts of information and research.
- Google: what would we do without you?
- Fabulous at Any Age: Harper's Bazaar
- How to have style: Isaac Mizrahi
- The One Hundred: Nina Garcia
- The Little Black Book of Style: Nina Garcia
- The Encyclopedia of Fashion: Georgina O'Hara

And countless blogs and magazines that I have scoured through the years for tools, tricks, tips and shortcuts on this fabulous style journey!

www.ingramcontent.com/pod-product-compliance
Lightning Source LLC
Chambersburg PA
CBHW040457240426
43665CB00039B/75